What Belongs to Us As Believers

HEATHER M. BATES

WESTBOW
PRESS®
A DIVISION OF THOMAS NELSON
& ZONDERVAN

WestBow Press books may be ordered through booksellers or by contacting:

WestBow Press
A Division of Thomas Nelson & Zondervan
1663 Liberty Drive
Bloomington, IN 47403
www.westbowpress.com
1 (866) 928-1240

ISBN: 978-1-5127-5670-8 (sc)
ISBN: 978-1-5127-5671-5 (hc)
ISBN: 978-1-5127-5669-2 (e)

Library of Congress Control Number: 2016915014

Print information available on the last page.

WestBow Press rev. date: 10/24/2016

Contents

Acknowledgments vii

Dedication ix

A Special Thank You to the Editor..xi

Introduction...xiii

Chapter 1   Endless Love...1

Chapter 2   The Spirit of an Overcomer 7

Chapter 3   Faith...13

Chapter 4   Creative Words 17

Chapter 5   The Holy Spirit..21

Chapter 6   A Rich Inheritance...31

Chapter 7   Rights as Kings and Priests 35

Chapter 8   The Mind of Christ 41

Chapter 9   Gifts 47

Chapter 10   A Glorious Future..57

Chapter 11   Ultimate Dominion 61

Chapter 12   Prosperity 65

Chapter 13   Made Alive 73

Chapter 14   Desire to Be a Giver..89

Acknowledgments

First and foremost, I credit ALL the honor and glory for this book to my Heavenly Father, who has both inspired and helped me to write this book in a timely manner. Even in the midst of constantly managing a home, filled with six dynamic children, He was always with me to help see this project through. Otherwise, had I needed to find the "spare time" to write this book under the sofa cushions, more than likely I would have found socks instead!

A close second to my Heavenly Father when it comes to credit due is Jonathan, the man I am honored to call my husband! The burden of all financial responsibilities of our lives weighs on him -- a decision he selflessly made when we got married. He always wanted me to be free from any financial stress and to have the ability to be the wife and mother God was calling me to be. I am forever grateful for that decision. As I have told him countless times, I would never want to trade places with him. I honor him as the head of our home and know his heart for our family.

Jonathan has supported me through the process of writing this book and has always been the BIG DREAMER of our family - encouraging me to press on with the assignments God has put on my life. I love you, Jonathan, and I am truly excited for the life of adventure that I know you are providing for our family!

Dedication

For those precious people out there in the mass of humanity who know they were created for a specific purpose and are actively searching for what that purpose is.

Also, for those wondering exactly what does belong to them when they become believers. Those who are tired of simply floating along in life, chalking up each sunrise as "just another day."

My prayer is that every person will grab ahold of the principles in this book and be able to create the life God designed for them to have.

There is so much life to live and so little time to live it!

A Special Thank You to the Editor

I would like to offer a special thank you to my brother-in-law, Harry Bates, Jr., for editing this book. His attention to detail and strong grasp of the English language made him the perfect person for this job. He has dedicated countless hours to making sure this book simply and effectively communicates the intended message.

Harry is not only Jonathan's brother, but also his best friend and business partner. I also want to mention that among the many hats Harry wears, one of the most special hats is his Uncle Harry hat! He has a HUGE heart for our children, and they are always excited to spend time with him!

Harry is a very special part of our family, and we love him so much!

Introduction

The twenty minute long message I had selected began to play on my iPhone as I held the speaker side of my phone to my ear. Even with the volume turned all the way up, this was the only way to listen, as I began the three-hour drive to my mom's house in Delaware this past Christmas day. All 6 children were settled in the Suburban and excited to visit Gramma for a few days! Ok, "settled" might not be the right word to use here.

Hence, the need for the phone to touch my ear. Even with a DVD movie playing, random conversations were happening between the 3 and 5-year-old girls, the 8-year-old girl complaining about the 7-year-old boy farting, and the 7-month-old baby making happy screeching sounds. Our oldest, newly-turned 13-year-old was my co-pilot, and with his amazing ability to focus on *any* media, seemed to be completely blocking out the other noises.

Every message that I hear blesses me, but this one had me hanging on every word and even replaying it two more times. Was it possible to find out everything that our Father has given us? I found myself saying out loud, "I wish there was a book out there listing out exactly what is available to us as believers."

Right away in my spirit I heard God say, "Why don't you write one?!" My immediate answer was, "Ok, I'll do it!"

My excitement about this new assignment made the rest of the trip to Gramma's house fly by. I knew this book was totally going to be God's work, considering I had barely enough hours in each day to keep the laundry caught up! The commercial-sized washer and dryer we had just picked out for our new home would be a big help, but they still required me to do the loading and unloading!

We had just finished celebrating Christmas with Jonathan's parents and brother, with multitudes of packed boxes accompanying us in our living room. Paper products had been stocked up to use in place of the dishes that were now all packed away, and Christmas break was well under way. This phase of our lives was truly a milestone for us, and would not be soon forgotten.

Even though we had spent the entire month of November packing to move into our first home on December 31st, this annual Christmas visit to my mom's was a do not miss! With every fiber of my being I wanted our family to move out of the tiny 1,200 square foot townhome that we had been renting for the past five years. No amount of work (and preparation) or holiday craziness could stop me from beginning work to make this dream of a heaven-sent book a reality!

Chapter 1

Endless Love

John 16:15 was the verse that had caught my attention that day, during my drive to visit my mom in Delaware. Jesus said, "All things that the Father has is mine, therefore I take what's mine and show it unto you." Jesus said He would show us everything our Father has given us. What exactly does our inheritance entail?

A study into God's Word will reveal everything the Father has that belongs to each of us—an heir. A joint heir. The first thing that comes to mind that the Father has and really *is*, is Love.

Everything else that we have hangs on love. We are told in 1 John 4:8 and 16 that God is love. God showed us how much He loved us by sending His only begotten son, Jesus, into our world, that we might live through Him (John 3:16), and that we might love through Him (1 John 4:9).

When we love, we look just like Jesus. Imagine that … our demeanor actually changes depending on how we act! We literally look different when we love someone as opposed to when we mistreat someone. God equipped us to love like Jesus when He shed His love abroad in our hearts by the Holy Ghost, which is given to us (Rom. 5:5). This allows us to walk in love at all times.

On the other hand, a whole book could be written on what God hasn't given us. In Deuteronomy 28, the list of curses is actually longer than the list of blessings. But the root of the curses is fear. That's the number-one thing that does not come from God. It is explained in 2 Timothy 1:7 that "God has not given us the spirit of fear, but of power and of love and of a sound mind."

Those things have been made a part of our spirit (who we are). How comforting to know that God has given us a sound mind! An estimated 26.2 percent of Americans ages eighteen and older (one in four adults) suffer from a diagnosable mental disorder every year. This translates to over fifty-seven million people in the United States alone (thekimfoundation.org). The number-one weapon to overcome this is God's Word. God gave us His Word so that we can use it as a handbook to solve all of life's problems.

The Word was God; the Word became flesh (Jesus) and dwelled among us (John 1:1&14). How thankful we should be that God gave us His Word, the Bible. It contains His love letters to us, our inheritance, His written will to us -- His children. Everything that He has purposed in His heart to give us can be found there. He, in turn desires for us to live the same way.

2 Corinthians 9:7 tells us that every man should give as he purposes in his heart to give -- not grudgingly, or of necessity, for God loves a cheerful giver.

The summer of 2005 found me at a point in my life that felt hopeless. It had been three years since I had last visited a church. I had been living only for myself, but something burst in me at the end of a church service when I heard an invitation to rededicate my life to my Father. I was overwhelmed by how much God still loved me and how much He desired to have a relationship with me.

I didn't know a soul at this church, but that didn't matter; I had just been reunited to my first love! Through a flood of tears, I committed the rest of my life to serving God.

I was overwhelmed by how much God still loved me and how much He desired to have a relationship with me.

Only a couple of weeks prior, I had been at the Salvation Army in York, Pennsylvania, gathering my weekly allotment of bread and other foods to supplement groceries for me and my two-and-a-half-year-old son. The food stamps the government gave us didn't quite meet our needs. I was a single mom, and every day was a struggle—especially since I was trying to do everything on my own, constantly putting out fires.

The lady who was helping me at the Salvation Army had a little plaque on her desk that said something about God, and I commented that I liked what it said. She asked me what church I attended, and I responded that I hadn't been to church in a long time. She recommended I visit her church. That church is where I recommitted my life to God.

It was also during this time that I was desperately looking to move out of my roach-infested apartment in downtown York, to a better place for my little boy. Although I was thankful that the government was helping me pay my rent and that we had a place of our own, I couldn't believe I had gotten myself into this situation. Nobody in my sphere of influence growing up could have predicted this would be my life by the time I turned twenty.

I had accepted Jesus into my heart as a five-year-old girl and was raised in a great home. I graduated from high school with my mom as my teacher, home-schooling me all of those years. Yet even with that solid foundation, I still somehow decided there had to be more to life than just what my parents had taught me. I was determined to find out for myself what else was out there instead of just believing what they had taught me to be the best way to live.

Sitting in my dingy apartment one day shortly after that church service, I made a deal with God that if He opened up a nice place for us to live, I would quit smoking cigarettes for good (a terrible habit I had picked up three years earlier).

Within just a couple of weeks, I got connected through the local newspaper with a Christian landlord who, to my great surprise, attended the church I was now attending! The landlord had a duplex in a nice, quiet neighborhood in the suburbs. There were mature trees along the sidewalks instead of neighborhood crime-watch signs and trash. The landlord even accepted Section 8, the housing program I was using so I could afford to pay the rent!

We moved into our new home right away -- a beautiful two-bedroom duplex with a yard and a garage in a peaceful neighborhood. This felt like luxury! It even came with a washer and dryer so my son and I didn't have to go to a Laundromat anymore!

I quit smoking before moving in and have never smoked since. God had held up His end of the deal, and I was surely going to hold up mine! I bought a notebook (not a nice journal) and began a new journey with God.

When we are filled with the revelation of how much God loves us, we will have the desire to give. God designed us to give the way He gives. He is the *ultimate* giver and desires for us as His children to act the way He acts.

Ephesians 3:17–19 encourages us to be rooted and grounded in love, that we may have strength to comprehend with all the saints what is the breadth and length and height and depth of God's love, and to know the love of Christ that surpasses mere human knowledge; that we may be filled with all the fullness of God.

Every moment we spend time with Him, we become more full of His love. A continual filling is necessary so we can keep giving His love to others.

Chapter 2

The Spirit of an Overcomer

We can fully walk in our inheritance when we live as overcomers. Jesus said, "To him that overcomes will I grant to sit with me in my throne." "He that overcomes shall inherit *all* things; and I will be his God and he shall be my son." We must live as overcomers, if we expect to tap into our inheritance (Rev. 2:17, 2:26, 3:12, 3:21, 21:7).

We can receive the spirit of an overcomer when we realize God has freely given us all things (Rom. 8:32). Freely! None of these things do we have to earn. God gives us richly all things to enjoy (1 Tim. 6:17).

How do we live as overcomers? Who do we overcome?

Revelation 12:10-11 says we overcome Satan. For those who permit it, Satan holds dominion over this world, and as such is the reason for everything negative that happens around us. The sooner we can recognize who the true enemy in this world is, the sooner we can understand whom we are fighting against. And we do that fighting by the blood of Jesus and the word of our testimony. The book, "The Blood and the Glory" by Dr. Billye Brim, in my opinion, is the best book on the blood of Jesus and how to use our authority as believers.

Living lives as total overcomers is God's desire for us. Making that happen every day is our choice. God has given every person a free will and the gift of choice (Deut. 30:14-16,19).

We can fully walk in our inheritance when we live as overcomers.

And on top of that, God has even told us which choices to make. How simple is that?! Nothing is complicated with God. His instructions for living as overcomers are spelled out clearly in His Word. The simple formula for discovering God's plans for us is in Deuteronomy 30:14. "The Word is very near unto us, in our mouth and in our heart that we may do it."

This is the process for both believers and non-believers. Whatever goes into our mind and heart comes out of our mouth and becomes our reality. It is important to understand clearly that this law abides equally, for good or bad. So in order to open up the life of an overcomer, we must diligently study God's Word, so that it dwells in our minds and hearts.

Then by default it will start coming out of our mouths (Matt. 12:34, Luke 6:45). Jesus has already overcome the world and set the example for us to follow (John 16:33). All we need to do is look to Jesus.

As Dr. Bill Winston says, "Jesus is the sample son." The first of many sons and daughters. Praise God that Jesus isn't the only begotten son anymore but that we too have an opportunity to become sons and daughters of God and take our place with Him! When we walk in His steps we automatically become overcomers. Romans 8:37 says we are more than conquers through Him who loved us. Through *Jesus*. More than conquerors!

John reassures us in 1 John 4:4 that because we are from God, we have overcome; because "greater is He who is in you than he who is in the world" (1 John 5:5). What a wonderful promise this is!

In addition to this passage, Revelation 2:7 sheds light in a bit of a different way on what an overcomer has access to. Jesus says, "To him that overcometh will I give to eat of the tree of life, which is in the midst of the paradise of God." In the Garden of Eden, Adam had access to the tree of life, giving him eternal life. This tree symbolizes righteousness and wisdom throughout the Bible. The Jews even call God's Word the "tree of life". "(Torah scrolls are) written on parchment, sewn together, rolled onto wooden rollers called eytz chayeem (tree of life), and read regularly in the synagogue."

Reference: Israel My Glory, May/June 2001, 23. How wonderful to know, now, that our tree of life is the cross!

One of the things I overcame was worrying about how Jonathan was leading our family. My biggest struggle after getting married was trusting God to lead our family through Jonathan. He was struggling with our finances (which is understandable, considering he had never been a husband or a father before) and as a result, we got evicted from our second home after getting married. Our second child was a few months old and I was pregnant with our third. We were being forced to move in with Jonathan's parents and older brother.

It was very easy during this time to become bitter toward Jonathan, and over time I allowed unforgiveness to fester in me even though I was spending time in God's Word. After giving birth to our third child, Andrew, instead of bringing our new baby to our home I had to bring him to Jonathan's parents' home.

I know God was speaking; we just weren't listening.

My breakthrough from worrying about our lives improving came when I discovered intercessory prayer and praying in the Spirit. Finally, I did have a part to play and a chance to put into practice what I had been learning over the past couple years.

I found my weapon against all of the attacks against my husband and our home.

I began praying very specific prayers and the day after praying, Jonathan would tell me about an "interesting" encounter he had that spoke to him … I found my weapon against all of the attacks against my husband and our home. Intercessory prayer… so simple, yet so powerful!

Chapter 3

Faith

Another thing God has given us is the measure of faith (Rom. 12:3). Without faith, it's impossible to please God. The faith of God was planted in us when we made Jesus the Lord of our lives.

Ephesians 3:12 says that our faith in Jesus allows us to have boldness and confidence when we access our Father. Because of the faith of God in us, we come boldly and confidently into God's presence. The message translation says, "We're free to say whatever needs to be said, bold to go wherever we need to go."

That measure of faith is already in us, waiting for us to put it into action to work for us. We first used this faith through grace when we accepted Jesus into our hearts. 1 Peter 1:1 says, "We have obtained like precious faith." Ephesians 4:7 says "Unto every one of us is given grace according to the measure of the gift of Christ."

"We are filled with all the fullness of God" (Eph. 3:19). Everything that God has is in us and working through us when we activate it. We must not allow God's power in us to lie dormant. Jesus paid too high a price at Calvary for us to ignore everything that is in us, trying to live life based solely on our own human strength.

We must not allow God's power in us to lie dormant.

As new creatures in Christ, *all things* are become new (2 Cor. 5:17). We will do the works of Jesus when we have faith or believe in the power that is at work in us (Eph. 3:20 and Phil. 2:13).

Just a couple days after being filled with the Holy Spirit, I asked God if there was something He wanted me to do or change and He told me that I needed to forgive. At that time I couldn't imagine whom I might have unforgiveness toward so I asked God, and right away He said I had unforgiveness toward my Dad.

My thoughts wandered back to ten years prior, when I had just given birth to my first child -- a boy. I had lived single and unwed in a maternity home my entire pregnancy. This Christian home was the place I needed to be at the time -- a positive environment three hours away from the situation in which I had put myself.

Unfortunately, just a couple weeks after Matthew was born, my Dad informed me in a conversation over the phone of his disapproval of the choices I had been making. His tone and intensity were totally devastating to me! After hanging up, I decided I didn't need him in my life. Even three years after that phone call, I didn't invite him to my wedding!

So that same day, when God told me to forgive, I called my dad's mother to get his number, and then ended up leaving him a message. The next day he called me back!

I told my dad what God had spoken to me about my unforgiveness; that I now forgave him for the hurtful words he had spoken to me so many years before.

After hanging up the phone from a fairly short conversation, I realized I was flooded with love and the lightest feeling I had experienced in a long time, the freeing feeling that only forgiveness can bring!

Over the past couple years now I have been able to spend precious time with my dad, and now our children are having a great relationship with their grandpa!

Our God is a God of restoration!

Strife must be flushed out of our relationships, if we are to progress the way God intended. God has given us a spirit of unity and we must operate in that constantly (Eph. 4:3 & 13).

As verse thirteen in the message translation says, "We are to all be moving

God has given us a spirit of unity.

rhythmically and easily with each other; efficient and graceful in response to God's son; fully mature adults."

Psalm 133:1 & 3 says, "Blessing and life come from living in unity with each other."

Jesus wants and needs us to be filled with His fullness so that His works can go forth in righteousness and power (Eph. 1:22-23).

Chapter 4

Creative Words

What does the Father have that belongs to us? The power to call things that be not as though they were. The power to look at a situation the way it is and say what God says about the situation instead of what it looks like in the natural.

For example, when our car breaks down and we know we didn't put extra money in the bank to cover emergencies, we turn to God's Word to find out what to say. Instead of saying, "I can't believe I'm without a car now! I don't know how I'm going to get to work, and my daughter has an important game tomorrow I have to be at…"

Open up God's Word and start saying what it says about the matter which is:

> My God supplies all my need according to His riches in glory by Christ Jesus. I do not worry saying, what shall I eat, or what shall I drink, or what shall I wear [or what shall I drive]? But I seek the kingdom of God above all else… and he will give me everything I need (Phil. 4:19, Matt. 6:31).

I like to personalize verses so they speak directly *to* me *about* me by saying "I do not worry saying 'what will I eat or what will I drink…?'." By lining our words up with His, God can get on the scene and work to line things up on our behalf.

We also have the power to name. Names are important to God. In biblical days, the Jewish people put serious thought and prayer into naming their children. They knew the name would determine who the child would become. The actual naming of the child was done before a congregation followed by a celebratory meal.

God set the example for us by giving each of the stars in the sky a name. Billions and billions of stars, each with a unique name, and God hasn't forgotten any of them!
"He tells the number of the stars; he calls them all by their names (Psalm 147:4)."

Lift up your eyes on high and see who has created these heavenly bodies; The One who brings out their host by number, He calls them all by name; because of the greatness of His might and the strength of His power, not one is missing (Isa. 40:26 Amp).

And even more importantly, He knows *us* by name. He gave Adam the authority **He knows us by** to name all of the animals at creation. **name.** Psalm 33:6 says, "By the Word of the Lord the Heavens were made. And by the breath of His mouth, all their hosts were made." A study of our massive solar system gives us a glimpse into how magnificent God is and how detailed He is. A brief read on NASA's website will leave us in awe of how massive, yet detailed God is.

In 1950, a Dutch astronomer named Jan Oort predicted the existence of a cloud consisting of icy debris. This is a thick bubble that surrounds our solar system. Nobody has actually seen the Oort cloud because of how vast it is. It's going to take NASA's Voyager 1 spacecraft 300 years to reach the inner surface of the Oort cloud, and then another 30,000 years to travel through to its outer surface. And to think that astronomers have named this region of space and it hasn't even officially been seen yet! How massive our universe is, and how much greater still is our Father!

Chapter 5

The Holy Spirit

Another thing that belongs to us as believers is the Holy Spirit. The best way for us to discover what our Heavenly Father has for us is to allow the Holy Spirit to be our teacher. We will never fully comprehend the things that God has prepared for us until we let the Holy Spirit reveal them unto us.

The Spirit searches out everything and shows us God's deep secrets.

The Holy Spirit searches all the deep mysteries of God; "his Spirit searches out everything and shows us God's deep secrets." (1 Cor. 2:10 NLT). The only reason they are secrets is because they must be hidden from the Devil so he won't interfere with our lives and God's plans for us.

Therefore, he won't interfere unless we let him, by speaking contrary to God's Word or living after the customs of this fleshly world. According to Ephesians 3:9, Paul was graced to make all men see God's mysteries, which from the beginning of the world had been hidden in God. 1 Corinthians 2:7 confirms that God ordained this hidden wisdom for us before the world was even created!

This mystery of God, God's wisdom, was previously hidden so that the devil would not know God's plan to send Jesus for us—for if he had known, he would not have crucified the Lord of glory (1 Cor. 2:8). This glorious, mysterious plan had to be hidden from the devil, and hidden for us and our benefit.

This wonderful plan was never hidden from us, which some people unfortunately believe. God's plan and His heart's desire since the foundation of the world has been to *give*. He is the ultimate giver. He gave and gave and gave all throughout history until His most precious gift was given, His only begotten Son, Jesus, whom he gave to be crucified on a cross as sacrifice for humanity's sins past, present, and future. He did this so we could walk in all the fullness of God (Matt. 7:11, Luke 11:13, James 1:17).

Ephesians 3:19 (AMP) tells us, "That we may be filled unto all the fullness of God, may have the richest measure of the divine presence, and become a body wholly filled and flooded with

God Himself." Ephesians 4:13 states, "That we all come into the knowledge of the Son of God, unto a perfect man, unto the measure of the stature of the fullness of Christ." The Amplified version of this verse is perfectly clear: "That we might arrive at really mature manhood (the completeness of personality which is nothing less than the standard height of Christ's own perfection)." Isn't that our hearts' desire?

That's how God sees us and expects us to live every day! Since He is the ultimate giver, He would never hide anything from us. Just as a parent would never hide any keys to success from their children.

A parent's main goal is to equip them to the best of their ability, to be prepared to flourish as an adult in this world. Again in Matthew 7:11, Jesus said, "If you then, being sinful know how to give good gifts to your children, how much more shall your Father give good things to them that ask Him?" So, when the Holy Spirit is our teacher, it is easy for us to learn! Especially since we have the mind of Christ (1 Cor. 2:16).

After I received the filling of the Holy Spirit in November of 2009, I began my journey in hearing from God through the Holy Spirit. Before that time, I had never actually heard from God in my spirit. All through my growing up years I felt close to God, and loved the time I spent with Him, but I had never actually heard God answer me when I asked Him

> *Since He is the ultimate giver, He would never, ever hide anything from us.*

a question. I had never heard Him speak anything to me from His Spirit to mine.

For me, after praying with a leader from our church one Sunday in November, I didn't see any physical change or manifestation like other people experience. I didn't immediately start speaking in tongues or fall on the floor in a trance. I went home that day with a little booklet to help me learn about what had just happened to me. I was so excited and felt like I couldn't get enough of God's Word, which I was seeing now in a whole new light!

Verses that I had known from memory since I was a little girl were jumping off the pages and for the first time, like Ephesians 1 says, the eyes of my understanding were being enlightened. After just a couple days, I did start praying in tongues and that aspect of my prayer life has increased ever since. What an awesome adventure this was!

In the summer of 2010, I was spending time with God, knowing in my spirit for weeks that a change was about to happen. I sensed that we needed to move to a different area but had no idea where we would move since we were completely settled in our life in Lancaster, PA. Our business team was there and growing. Most of our friends and family were in this same area. But inside of both myself and Jonathan was a strong desire to move on. So we determined to seek God and find out exactly what to do.

Within several days I heard God say "Michigan" when I asked where we should move. Of course, I asked for confirmation, since Michigan is eleven hours from where we lived!

I heard "Grand Rapids" and the more I prayed, the more confirmation I got. Pictures of rapids, rushing water... everything I received pointed to Michigan. So, of course, my next thought was to tell Jonathan that I had heard from God but to not tell him what I had heard. I wanted to find out what he received when he prayed to find out if we were on the same page.

So he spent time by himself to pray about where God wanted us to move. Twenty minutes later he came to me and told me he had clearly heard where we should move. He said he heard one word from God and it was "Michigan!" As much as I was surprised, I was not surprised, considering how sure I was of what God had been telling me. Excitement filled my entire being. I immediately took Jonathan to my journal where I had written all about Michigan the past week and let him read.

He was shocked and I knew this would be a journey as we continued to seek God for specifics. I knew every detail of this move needed to be directed by God for it to work out to be the amazing plan He intended. God knew we were capable of hearing him for this assignment and carrying it out, which was a super humbling thought to me. I was excited beyond explanation!

Jonathan was cautious. He's always been the kind of person who needed to see everything drawn out before making a move.

He will tell you himself that he has lived by the Boy Scout motto: "Be Prepared."

Right away we told our landlord that we would be moving within a month, and by the end of that month most of our belongings were in a storage unit and we were temporarily living with Jonathan's parents. He and I and our three children, me being almost due with our fourth, all lived in one bedroom since his brother also lived with his parents in the third bedroom of the three-bedroom split level home. Jonathan was still working in Lancaster (fifty minutes from his parents' home) and I was spending my spare minutes, when our two younger ones were napping, listening to further instruction from God.

Days turned into weeks, which turned into months. Finally, five months after moving into his parents' house, Jonathan found a duplex in the Grand Rapids area for us to move into. With no job lined up and no further direction in any other area (only because there wasn't enough time invested in seeking for direction), we packed a big U-Haul, including everything from our storage unit. Early on a Saturday morning, at the beginning of February, we set off for Michigan.

Since our youngest was only 4 months old, the 11-hour trip turned into a 15-hour trip, with us arriving at our new home around one in the morning. Our new landlord, gracious as he was, met us at that insane hour of the night to give us our new keys and we toted sleeping little ones inside to spend the rest of the night on the floor.

Upon waking up relatively early, since we planned to go to church to start this new adventure off right, I spent the first of my waking minutes with Jesus. How thankful I was for this new chapter of our lives and genuinely excited about what God had in store for us.

My excitement turned to shock as Jonathan came and informed me that he thought we didn't belong in Michigan and should immediately move back to PA!

Satan wasn't wasting any time trying to convince us that what we were doing was crazy and irresponsible. A lot of times assignments God gives us will not make sense right away, which is where our faith

It doesn't have to make sense; it has to make faith.

is given a chance to work. Something we learned down the road was that it doesn't have to make sense; it has to make faith. After going to church followed by lunch, instead of unpacking we spent hours wrestling between our calling and our doubts.

The next morning, with all of our belongings still in the U-Haul, we started our trip back to Pennsylvania. My heart was broken, knowing what we were doing was not right but not having any other answers. I knew we would never know what God had in store for us in Michigan.

When we arrived back in Lancaster, PA, we ended up in a hotel for several days, while we desperately looked for a place to rent. Our income tax refund was about drained, along with most of the rent the landlord in Michigan had graciously given us back.

We had paid six months rent upfront to secure our duplex, since Jonathan didn't have a job lined up at that time. After living close to a week in a hotel, we signed the lease on a two-bedroom townhome and moved in right away.

Little did we know that we would be living there for the next five years! It's crazy how we make life so hard, when the Holy Spirit is waiting all the time to tell us exactly what to do to guide us through life. All we have to do is be willing to spend some time with Him, to develop that intimate relationship.

The Holy Spirit is so many things to us …

The Holy Spirit guides us into all truth- John 16:8

He regenerates us- John 3:5-8

He glorifies us and testifies of Christ- John 15:26, 16:14

He leads us- Rom.8: 14, Gal. 5:18

He empowers us- Luke 4:14, Rom. 15:19, Acts 1:8

He teaches us to pray- Rom. 8:26-27, Jude 1:20

He bears witness that we are children of God- Rom. 8:16

He produces in us the fruit or evidence of His work and presence- Gal. 5:22-23

He distributes spiritual gifts and manifestations- 1 Cor. 12:4, 8-10

He is our guarantee of the future resurrection- 2 Cor. 1:22

He sets us free from the law of sin and death- Rom. 8:2

He quickens our mortal bodies- Rom. 8:11

He reveals the deep things of God to us- 1 Cor. 2:10

HE REVEALS WHAT HAS BEEN GIVEN TO US

FROM GOD- 1 Cor. 2:12

He dwells in us- Rom. 8:9

He speaks to us and through us- 1 Cor. 12:3, 1 Tim. 4:1, Rev. 2:11

He brings liberty- 2 Cor. 3:17

He transforms us into the image of Christ- 2 Cor. 3:18

He enables us to wait- Gal. 5:5

He grants us everlasting life- Gal. 6:8

He gives us access to God- Eph. 2:18

He makes us God's Habitation- Eph. 2:20

He reveals the mystery of God- Eph. 3:5

He strengthens our spirit- Eph. 3:16

He enables us to obey the truth- 1 Pet. 1:22

He dispenses God's love into our hearts- Rom. 5:5

He teaches us- 1 Cor. 2:13

He gives us joy- 1 Thess. 1:6

He enables us to preach the gospel- Pet. 1:12

He moves us- 2 Pet. 1:21

He casts out demons- Matt. 12:28

He brings things to our remembrance- John 14:26

He comforts us- Acts 9:31

Chapter 6

A Rich Inheritance

Something else God has given us is a rich inheritance. "The inheritance in us is rich and glorious" (Eph. 1:18).

Psalm 16:5 puts it this way: "The Lord is the portion of mine inheritance and of my cup: You maintain my lot." The Webster's definition of portion is "An individual's part or share of something. A share received by gift or inheritance; an individual's lot, fame or fortune." What a wonderful definition!

The inheritance God has given each of us truly is a gift. There's no way any of us could have earned it. Verse six continues by saying, "I have a good heritage." The NLT says, "You guard all that is mine." The MSG adds, "You set me up with a house and a yard. Then you made me your heir!" God even cares about the details of our lives such as our house and yard!

Psalm 94:14 reassures us that "The Lord will not cast off His people, neither will He forsake His inheritance." There's no way we can lose our inheritance! It's eye opening to see that wisdom is considered to be equal to our inheritance. A lack of wisdom will only see to it that our inheritance is squandered throughout our lifetime.

> Wisdom is as good as an inheritance and by it there is profit to them that see the sun [those still alive] (Eccl. 7:11).

"God and the word of His grace is able to build you up and to give you an inheritance among all them that are sanctified" (Acts 20:32). Our Father has qualified us to share the portion, which is the inheritance of the saints in the Light (Col. 1:12). "We are promised an eternal inheritance which will never fade away" (Heb. 9:15 & 1 Pet. 1:4).

How do we know this is true? Ephesians 1:13-14 tells us "The Holy Spirit is God's guarantee that He will give us the inheritance He promised and that He

The Holy Spirit is the down payment on our heritage.

purchased us to be His own people." The Holy Spirit is the down payment on our heritage.

We already saw in Chapter 5 everything the Holy Spirit is to us. Take a minute and think about that… the Holy Spirit is the down payment on our heritage. Webster's dictionary defines heritage as: "An estate that passes from an ancestor to an heir by course of law."

Just as the size of the down payment on a house determines the size of the house, so the bigness of the Holy Spirit gives us a glimpse of the glory of what is to come when Heaven becomes our permanent home!

What a wonderful and impactful revelation this is to me, considering we just bought our first home less than one month ago as I write this! We saw how true that was as we looked at many different homes. The cheaper the home was, the fewer luxuries it contained.

The Bible also says that we as believers are earthen vessels. In ancient days people put important documents in earthen vessels so they would last a long time (Jer. 32:14). As we hide God's words in our hearts, they are preserved there. Psalm 12:6 says, "The words and promises of the

If we would fully grasp the power in the words of God we would never let a morning go by where we didn't spend time immersing ourselves in His words!

Lord are pure words, like silver refined in an earthen furnace, purified seven times over." *Wow!*

If we would fully grasp the power in the words of God we would never let a morning go by where we didn't spend time immersing ourselves in His words!

Chapter 7

Rights as Kings and Priests

What else does our inheritance entail? When we receive Jesus as our Lord and Savior, He makes us Kings and Priests unto God. As Kings, we rule and reign.

Old Webster's dictionary (1828) defines a king as: "A man invested with supreme authority over a nation or country. Kings are hereditary sovereigns when they hold the powers of government by right of birth or inheritance."

As Priests, we pray. The definition of a priest is a licensed minister of the gospel. A priest is a mediatory agent between people and God. An intercessor.

Christ is called the king of his church. Psalm 2, especially verse eight, reveals how God gave Jesus the nations as His inheritance and the uttermost parts of the earth as His possession. Thank you, Jesus, for choosing us as your inheritors, so we can choose you as our inheritance! Oh, what love the Father has toward us that we should be called the sons and daughters of God (1 John 3:1, Rev. 5: 10, Rom. 8: 16-17).

God has made us kings and priests and we are to reign on the earth. We don't need to wait until we get to Heaven some day to reign. It's now, on this earth, where our authority needs to be exercised. In this compilation of titles, the king is supreme over the lives and property of men and the priest holds sway over the hearts and consciences of men. In this, nothing can escape from our dominion. Let me say it again, *nothing* can escape from our dominion!

Oh what love the Father has toward us that we should be called the sons and daughters of God.

Peter called us "a chosen generation, a royal priesthood." The Greek text (revised version) says, "He made us to be a kingdom and to be priests." Not only are we children of God but also heirs of God (Rom. 8:17). The 1828 Webster's dictionary defines heir as "the man on whom the law casts an estate of inheritance. A man's children are his heirs." "One who is entitled to possess, to take possession of."

We are heirs of the promise (all of God's covenant promises), heirs of righteousness (God's ways of doing and being right), heirs of salvation. This explains why so many believers live in lack and sickness and depression, and many other things that by default have come upon them. They haven't activated the inheritance inside of them. The exact same inheritance dwells inside every single child of God, but only when we take possession of it, and start acting like heirs and speaking like heirs, will it begin to manifest in our lives.

Romans 8:17 also adds that we are joint-heirs with Christ. The AMP says that we share Christ's inheritance with Him. Everything that Christ is, is also in us! In Acts 26:18 Jesus told Saul to preach so that the world would receive forgiveness of sins, and inheritance among them that are sanctified by faith in Jesus. Isn't this the commission all of us should receive and walk in?

Ephesians 1:11 reiterates, "Through Jesus, we have obtained an inheritance." The MSG says, "It's in Christ that we find out who we are and what we are living for."

Long before we first heard of Christ and got our hopes up, He had His eye on us; had designs on us for glorious living as part of the overall purpose He is working out in everything and everyone." Wow, this is a verse we ought to read over and over and really meditate on… it would change our lives!

As sons and daughters of God, we are heirs of God through Christ (Gal. 4:7). Galatians 3:29 also tells us that when we become

Christ's, then are we Abraham's seed and heirs according to the promise. Much can be discovered about what our inheritance entails by looking at what God promised Abraham. The list is long and every bit of it applies to us today, according to Galatians 3:29 and Galatians 3:16.

The promises begin in Genesis 12:1, where God says, "I will make of you a great nation and I will bless you and make your name great; and you will be a blessing and I will bless them that bless you and curse them that curse you, and in you will all families of the earth be blessed."

Righteousness is simply God's ways of doing and being right.

A long list of blessings continues in Deuteronomy 28:1-13. Verse two says not only will these blessings come on us, but they will also overtake us. I don't know about you, but I am fine with being overtaken by blessings!

Paul explains in Titus 3:7 that through Jesus, we are made heirs according to the hope of eternal life. The MSG clearly adds, "God's gift has restored our relationship with him and given us back our lives. And there's more life to come - an eternity of life! You can count on this." Jesus is heir of all things (Heb.1:2). We are heirs of salvation (Heb. 1:14). That makes us heir of all things.

Thus the purpose of this book -- to find out all the things that are ours as heirs.

We are heirs of the righteousness of God (Heb. 11:7). Righteousness is simply God's way of doing and being right. That righteousness is in us now. We are heirs of the Kingdom (James 2:5). God's Kingdom is a system of government established by God, with Jesus as its King. Jesus is the King of kings. He is King of us, since we have already seen that we are kings.

Imagine being able to live and operate in a heavenly kingdom here on this earth, where we don't have to be controlled by the government and its shortcomings. No matter where on this earth we live, this is how God created us to live - us controlling our circumstances, not our circumstances controlling us.

In the midst of the busyness of each day, we must slow down to remember that each day is a gift. Husbands and wives especially, as they go their separate ways each day, must remember that they are heirs together to the grace (or gift) of life (1 Pet. 3:7).

Let us never get so busy that we lose sight of the fact that this life is a gift from God. Ephesians 1:18 (NLT) reveals the rich and glorious inheritance God has given His holy people. *Everything the Father has belongs to us!*

So many people quote 1 Corinthians 2:9 which says "Eye has not seen, nor ear heard, neither have entered into the heart of man, the things which God has prepared for them that love him." If we only had our natural mind to depend on, this would be true but praise God that's not the end of the story! The next verse tells us that God reveals these things to us through his Spirit.

So, when the Holy Spirit is our teacher, it is easy for us to learn. Especially since we have the mind of Christ (1 Cor. 2:16). Let us set off today on a lifelong journey to learn!

Chapter 8

The Mind of Christ

When we made Jesus Lord of our lives, we became new creatures; old things passed away and all things became new (2 Cor. 5:17).

When we understand that we have the mind of Christ, it becomes an adventure to let the Holy Spirit begin to teach us God's mysteries. God has already prepared these things for us and is waiting with patient anticipation for us to come to Him to learn.

This is why we receive the Spirit, God's Spirit, so that we might know the things that are freely given to us by God. It is vital for us to keep our minds fixed on God all the time! Perfect peace, among countless other things, will surround us when our minds are fixed on God (Isa. 26:3, Col. 3:2, 2 Cor. 10:5). An excellent study on how to keep our minds in the right place is Joyce Meyers' book "Battlefield of the Mind."

As 1 Corinthians 2:12 says, we should know the things that are freely given to us by God. In searching the "things" that God has freely given us, let us keep in mind that God has given Himself to us. This may seem obvious, but take a minute to really dwell on this. More than ten times throughout the Bible, God tells us, "I will be their God."

1 Corinthians 3:22-23 in the MSG confirms that "Everything is already yours as a gift - Paul, Apollos, Peter, the world, life, death, the present, the future – all of it is yours, and you are privileged to be in union with Christ, who is in union with God."

We are filled with all the fullness of God (Eph. 3:19, John 1:16, Col. 2:9-10). As Joseph Prince pointed out, "Being filled with the fullness of God is not about what you do, but about knowing how much God loves you." Knowing the love of Christ and focusing on God's love for us is what confirms to us that we are filled with God.

God is love. We must constantly feed on God's love for us. As we do this, we will be supernaturally filled with the fullness of God.

"Being filled with the fullness of God is not about what you do, but about knowing how much God loves you."

What a simple process... all it takes on our part is believing His love, and being disciplined enough to feed on God's love every day!

As we meditate on God's love for us we also see that God is light (1 John 1:5).

God's light is shed on our lives and paths when we spend time reading and meditating on His Word (Ps. 119:130, John 1:4,5 and 9).

The entrance of God's Word gives light and understanding to us. Jesus told us in John 8:12 that "He is the light of the world" and when we follow Him we will have the light of life.

This is love -- God sent His only Son into the world so we might live through Him (1 John 4:10). When we love one another, God dwells deeply within us, and His love becomes complete in us -- perfect love! Perfected love then casts out all fear.

We ought to thank God every day that His love is shed abroad in our hearts because there sure are enough reasons to be fearful throughout the day. Ten minutes in front of the television, a newspaper or media driven magazine will invoke fear into anyone. Our society even equates fear with preparedness. There is actually such a thing as a "culture of fear."

Wikipedia defines this as "people inciting fear in the general public to achieve political goals." It also applies to the workplace, where employers use negative reinforcement, even exercising a tyrannical style of management.

Again, what we feed on develops our views of the world around us. If we spend hours every evening watching television, our outlook on life will be more negative. If we feed on God's Word every day, our views will be aligned with how God sees the world. Through eyes of compassion.

I was shocked recently, when I opened up my weekly email from our local library. There was an announcement of an upcoming event at the library called "Death Café." Readers were encouraged to join this group, to better prepare themselves for death and discuss a book written on the topic. There was even an invitation to meet with a death doula (imagine that being your profession)! And oh, by the way, there would be cake, cookies and coffee to help ease the depressing conversations.

Although death is not usually a pleasant topic, we should be encouraged to find out that it is not something that suddenly overtakes us. We as believers have the authority to reject or accept death. Throughout the Bible we can see many people who willfully agreed to die when they could have continued to live such as Jesus who "gave up the ghost" and Stephen who called out "receive my spirit". Too many people allow unfortunate situations to take them out, saying, "it must just be my time to go", when God is clear about every believer living a long, prosperous life.

It doesn't take an in-depth study of God's Word to find out that we've been raised from death unto life. We will only be able to positively influence this world when we are full of God's life and compassion. His heart is to see everyone come to know Him (1 Tim. 2:4).

The word "know" in the Greek is Cognosco, which is far more powerful than our current definition of the word. It goes far deeper than having an understanding of or being acquainted with. The deepest sense of the word is to have sexual relations with, as when Adam *knew* Eve.

This knowledge means that Adam knew everything there was to know about Eve. He knew more about her than anyone else would ever know. This is how our Heavenly Father desires us to know him - to clearly understand him.

We were created to know God that way. Through the Holy Spirit, who is called the Spirit of truth, He will guide us into *all* truth *and* show us things to come (John 16:13)!

The Holy Spirit searches the deep things of God and reveals them unto us (1 Cor. 2:10). Verse 9 of this same chapter says "Eye has not seen, not ear heard, neither have entered into the heart of man the things God has prepared for them that love Him." Just when we start to understand God's plans for us and who He is, He reveals more to us. This glorious process will continue throughout eternity.

What a wonderful future we have! We must not waste a single day doing things our own way or neglecting to feed on God's Word.

We are born from above. We are citizens of Heaven (John 3:3).

The Greek word "anothen," used to describe "born," includes two meanings. The first meaning has to do with position, "from above" (John 3:31, John 9:11, James 1:17).

The second meaning has to do with time -- when a baby is physically born. Jesus, in talking to Nicodemus in John 3:3, was obviously talking about being born from above. When we are born again,

We are born from above. We are citizens of Heaven.

or born from above, we automatically qualify for every good and perfect gift that is from above. It's time to receive those gifts!

Chapter 9

Gifts

Another way to look at everything the Father has that belongs to us is to find out the different gifts our Father has given to us. Romans 8:32 tells us, "God freely gives us all things." Proverbs 17:8 says "Whichever way we turn our gifts, they prosper." It is part of our nature to be givers, just like God is. We take pleasure in giving for all kinds of occasions. And if the average person is asked whether they enjoy giving a gift or receiving a gift, most will respond that giving is more fulfilling. This confirms what Jesus said in Acts 20:35, "It is more blessed to give than to receive."

Giving is a part of our nature given to us from our Father who is the ultimate teacher!

In the journal "Science," social psychologist Elizabeth Dunn showed that people were happier when they spent money on others as opposed to only on themselves. In a survey of over 600 American citizens, Dunn discovered that spending money on others produced greater happiness across all income levels. "Science" Mar. 21, 2008 Vol. 319, Issue 5870 pp. 1687-1688.

It is part of our nature to be givers just like God is.

Even other religions include teachings of giving, such as the Buddhist principle that says "One's own happiness is dependent on the happiness of others."

Mahatma Gandhi said, "The best way to find yourself is to lose yourself in the service of others." Jesus taught this same principal in Acts 20:35, where He said, "It is more blessed to give than to receive."

Winston Churchill once stated: "We make a living by what we get. We make a life by what we give."

There is a sense of pride that comes along with everything we own here on this earth. Whether it's a vehicle, a nice home or our belongings, we automatically have a desire to take care of those things and make sure they look their best.

We just purchased our first home and have noticed how differently we look at things now, than we did when we were renting. Even though as renters we did our best to take care of what God had blessed us with, we knew ultimately what we worked hard to keep nice didn't belong to us. As heirs of a King, how differently would we view life if we constantly kept in mind that we have ownership over everything!

"We make a living by what we get. We make a life by what we give."

Along with ownership comes a sense of responsibility, knowing that nobody but us is going to take care of our property. When we comprehend all that God has given us ownership or authority over, we will automatically want to cultivate and protect those things. We will be quick to keep the devil from interfering in our affairs. Just as Jonathan and I protect our new home with a top of the line security system, we must also protect our Heavenly ownerships.

We do this by watching how we speak and how others speak over us. How much power do our words carry? When our words line up with God's Word, they are powerful and sharper than any two-edged sword (Heb. 4:12).

Thank God we can choose which words to accept or reject that other people speak over us. If it doesn't line up with the Word of God, it doesn't belong in our lives and in our minds. If a doctor's report about us doesn't agree with what God's Word says about us, we simply reject those words and find scripture to stand on that will solve whatever the physical problem is.

We are thankful for doctors but we know that God's Word is final authority on any issue. This works with any problem the devil tries to put on us – emotional, psychological, etc.

God created us with the ability to use the same formula He used, when he created the earth in Genesis 1:1. The Spirit of God was hovering over the earth, waiting for God to speak out those creation words. Then the Spirit used those words to create (Gen. 1:2).

That same process works today... the Holy Spirit is always waiting for us to speak words that He can use to change our situations. We speak, the Holy Spirit moves, and those words become things that manifest (come to pass) in our lives.

We must understand that this process can also work against us, if we aren't speaking in line with God's Word. When we speak negative words, Satan is ready to make sure they happen. Through this process, we literally control what happens in our lives every day!

Through a little discipline, we can create the exact lives we want to live and that our Father wants us to live.

In learning about how God is the ultimate giver, and that He gave Jesus for us (John 3:16), it's interesting to note that 1 John 3:16 says exactly the same thing as John 3:16!

God, who is love, gave us Jesus, who is also love, because He loved us so and wanted us, His children, back in His family.

"God's love has been shed abroad in our hearts by the Holy Ghost ..." (Rom. 5:5); therefore, fear cannot exist in our hearts. Perfected love has cast out all fear (1 John 4:18).

A revelation of how much God loves us provides us the desire to give ourselves to others (2 Cor. 9:6-11). God has also given us the gift of prophesying, the gift of serving, the gift of teaching, encouraging, giving, leading, and showing mercy (Rom. 12:4-8). Still other gifts are of Faith, healing, miraculous powers, prophecy, distinguishing between spirits, and of speaking in and interpreting different tongues (1 Cor. 12:9-11).

Jesus also gave gifts unto men when He ascended to Heaven (Eph. 4:8). We must be faithful stewards of the gifts (graces) God has given us. We do this by serving others. Our speech matching God's Word, our actions done with the strength God provides (1 Peter 4:10-11).

God's love dwelling in us will automatically want to flow out of us as He designed. We are not meant to wander through life on our own. We are the body of Christ and therefore connected to each other. Just as the hand cannot work without the arm and shoulder, so believers are to operate, giving of ourselves for each other selflessly.

Our society has taught independence over the recent decades. Living self centered and independent of each other is not God's plan. Although we are not to be dependent on anyone, especially the government, to meet our needs or secure our future, we should let other believers into our lives so we can strengthen each other.

Why then, if our Father gives us richly all things to enjoy have we not been doing more enjoying? It seems we have been so caught up in "making a living" and tending to all of our things that the ultimate assignment on our lives has been pushed to the back burner.

If we could fully grasp and understand the power that is in us, ready to come out of us, we wouldn't hesitate to step out of our comfort zone and fulfill our hearts' desires.

God has given us His exceeding great power!

God has given us His exceedingly great power! The same power that raised Jesus from the dead and seated Him at the Father's right hand in Heavenly places.

When was the last time you did something that was truly your heart's desire to do?

Somebody recommended a book to me when I was pregnant with our fifth child, Madelyn. It was called "Supernatural Childbirth." When I starting reading this book, I had no idea it was even possible to give birth to a child without using any medication, while experiencing no pain. I had never heard anybody's testimony of this working, and definitely never heard any doctor or nurse mention this was possible.

I delivered my first child with the help of an epidural, thinking that would take away all pain. That was true until I started pushing. For three hours I was in tremendous pain as I struggled to deliver this baby, after all of the epidural had left my system! The doctors even discussed doing a C-Section that I was thankful didn't have to happen.

With our second child, I had decided to have the baby naturally (with no medication) and did stick to my plan even though later I questioned what in the world I was trying to prove! I did the same thing with our third and fourth children -- each of them coming naturally, but with lots of pain.

So when I started reading this book and found out that I could possibly give birth without medication AND without pain, I was very intrigued!

What I found was for this to work, I would have to go through God's Word and find out exactly what He had to say about this. I was happy to do so and, after reading the book many times over and believing with all my heart that this would work, I waited in excited anticipation for the big day, the day when this baby would let me prove to the world (well, at least my little world) that this would work!

This was also our only baby that we didn't find out whether it was a boy or girl ahead of time. Up to that point we had two boys and two girls, so we were content to be surprised by either blessing.

Finally, two days after my due date, my water broke.

This is exactly what I had prayed for, a sure sign that it was time to go to the hospital but that I would have plenty of time to get there and not be rushed. Of course I was already packed and ready to go!

Everything progressed smoothly and, after being in labor for six hours, I had still not experienced any pain. Then the moment of truth had come: it was time to push!

With each push I told my body and baby what to do and exercised my God given authority that I had learned during the previous months. After only ten minutes of pushing, a baby girl was born!

Through the final ten minutes I only felt pressure, never pain. The doctor and nurses were amazed at the whole process and I joined in their amazement when we found out this was our biggest baby yet, at nine pounds and one ounce!

I felt God's shining light of glory, in appreciation of the faith I had just put in Him! What an awesome testimony it was to share with the doctors and nurses, that God was the one who made it possible for me to give birth to a nine-pound baby with no medication *and* no pain! I wish I had known this was available when I was pregnant with our first baby, AND the second... third... fourth!

The birth of our sixth baby was the same supernatural process, with the blessing of another baby girl (this time we knew what to expect; Jonathan couldn't handle the suspense of waiting to find out again)!

How amazing it was to have a God-given desire in my heart and watch God bring it to fruition, as a result of my diligence in studying His Word and having faith that He would do what He said. God has truly given us His exceedingly great power... what a revelation!

That's why we can do the same things Jesus did, and even greater things still (John 14:12). This verse seems to be a mystery to many people, but it really isn't when God himself powers the things we're doing!

Chapter 10

A Glorious Future

Along with all of those good and perfect gifts also comes wisdom. This wisdom from above is pure, providing those who receive it with the characteristics of peace, love, gentleness, mercy and flexibility. It is the full fruit, resulting from the contribution of good deeds; never showing favoritism and is always sincere.

"All things that the Father has is mine," Jesus said. "Therefore, I will take what's mine and show it unto you." This wisdom

This wisdom will show us what is ours.

will show us what is ours. What exactly belongs to our Father that has been given to us.

It is really unfair to expect to be able to put into a book everything that the Father has that has been given to us. Many of the things that belong to us we will not even have access to until we get to Heaven. There are dimensions in Heaven that aren't even here on this earth!

Imagine cities that have streets of solid gold, (not just paved with gold... the whole street is solid gold), warmth of light without darkness, and an abundant variety of music; all of which praises our Father. Countless types of fruit abound in heaven, and are always producing.

We will never have concern for money, sickness, or disease. Our minds will never suffer from negativity or doubt; complete unity will be among everybody -- strife, non-existent. Tears and sadness will be a thing of the past and there will never be a shortage of God's glory.

How about being partnered with God to create things, including more planets and things beyond our imagination right now? How about being able to sit down and learn from some of the patriarchs down through history? Heaven, our soon to be home, is a wonderful place where all of these things and more abound. A place of complete comfort.

My mom is my go-to person for discussions about Heaven. You see, she has cerebral palsy, due to complications from being born three months before her due date. As a result of this, she has endured countless surgeries, including three beautiful ones when my two sisters and I were each born.

My mom has always had to use crutches to walk, which greatly limited her in being part of her children's active lives growing up. She endured social shuns, criticisms and frustrations and today has to deal with multiple additional physical challenges, as she ages.

In spite of all this, my mom has always put her Heavenly Father first in her life, and as a result is one of the most positive, cheerful, uplifting people you can meet! She also doesn't let having to use a wheelchair stop her from working a regular job.

For the last 14 years, with the use of special controls in her car, she has traveled to and from the job she started working, after having completed the many years of homeschooling her three daughters.

In all that time teaching, she never got paid, even though she could have made a good living with her BS in Psychology. She instead selflessly chose to sacrifice her talents to the greater good, her children's upbringing. But how great her reward will be in Heaven when her Father says, "Well done, good and faithful servant. You have been faithful over few, now I will make you ruler over many; enter now into the joy of the Lord!"

Most conversations with my mom about Heaven include her excitement of how she will be able to run when she gets

"In Serving One Another, We Become Free."

there. Somehow I don't think she will even notice those golden streets!

And even though she's lived on her own now for 15 years, dealing with all of her daily struggles alone, she cheerfully lives to serve. My mom would probably admit that she doesn't know the whole story of King Arthur from way back in the sixth century, but she follows his Knights of the Round Table's famous pledge, which reads, "In Serving One Another, We Become Free."

She is a free spirit and a joy to anyone who meets her!

We spend so much time and money making our earthly homes comfortable, when Jesus told us in John 14:2 that He has prepared our mansions for us in Heaven. Not just homes that meet our needs… *mansions!* The definition of a mansion is a place of residence, a habitation of the Lord of the land. The large house of a wealthy person.

That's us!

2 Corinthians 5:1 reminds us "If our earthly house of this tabernacle were dissolved, we have a building of God, a house not made with hands, eternal in the heavens." Our conversations should always be Heavenly centered (Phil. 3:20).

Chapter 11

Ultimate Dominion

One of my favorite passages describing what God has given us is Psalm 8. Verse 6 of that chapter says God made us to have dominion over the works of His hands and He puts ALL things under our feet. Everything from the land to the sky to the sea.

1 Corinthians 15:27, Ephesians 1:22-23 and Hebrews 2:6-8 also confirm this wonderful position we hold. Hebrews 2:8 goes even further to say that God left nothing outside of man's control and that at this time we do not even see all the things that are subjected to us... *wow!*

We will do well if we fully grasp and own the fact that *all* things are in subjection to us here on this earth. ALL things! Finances, health, position, influence, etc.

Finances were the one area of our lives that seemed would never get under control. Some people struggle living paycheck-to-paycheck… year after year we just wished we had a paycheck.

One summer, we had re-enrolled our three older children in their Christian school with no clue how we would pay for any of it. The electric company was again threatening to turn our electric off since we were behind over $2,000.

A few times it did get turned off, during the five years we lived in our two-bedroom townhome. Each time I would steer clear of all windows, not wanting to make eye contact with the guy shutting the electric off.

So our children started school at the Christian school and Cindy, the finance person, assured us that she would do everything she could to get us the most assistance possible. She knew we needed 100% assistance.

January rolled around and we had heard nothing and were now behind over $5,000. We decided just after the first of the year to take our kids to school and see if we could talk to their principle about our situation.

We were planning to tell him that we were going to teach our kids at home through cyber-school, because of our lack of finances. He happened to be in the hallway that morning and we were able to meet with him in his office. He is the kindest person and through our entire conversation conveyed his heart for our children to continue to attend the school, and told us that something would work out.

We left that morning encouraged but still with no idea how we would pay for our children's schooling, which was a daunting $19,400.00!

Finally one morning in mid-January, a phone call came in from the school. Cindy explained that the school board was not able to help with more than 40% of the tuition, but that her and her husband felt that God wanted them to pay for the remainder of the tuition… through the end of the school year!!

I cried! With tears flowing down my cheeks, I expressed my deep thankfulness. Cindy and her husband literally paid thousands of dollars to make it possible for our children to have the best education, during a season where it looked impossible for them to remain at that school.

During that same year, God had impressed on my heart to start a "thankful jar," where I wrote on pieces of paper every blessing God brought our way. That jar filled up quickly and I had a visual of the many ways God had supplied us.

There's an intricate web of events that God is constantly weaving for us.

On two different occasions, a $500 check randomly showed up in our mailbox. One was anonymous and the other from a friend who didn't even know our whole situation!

It still amazes me how God takes our prayers and speaks to certain people to answer those prayers. I call them divine connections.

An eye opening short read on how everything that happens in our lives is connected, is the book "The Butterfly Effect." I find that this book does a good job of illustrating to believers, that there's an intricate web of events that God is constantly weaving for us.

Chapter 12

Prosperity

One huge benefit of God's inheritance in us is the opportunity to prosper in every area of our lives. 3 John 2 says "Beloved, I wish above all things that you prosper and be in health, even as your soul prospers." We see right away that the key to us prospering and being in health is our soul prospering first.

Our soul (mind, will, and emotions) must be filled to overflowing with the attributes of God. What goes in will come out in abundance (out of the abundance of the heart the mouth speaks), and what comes out of our mouth creates our world.

The dictionary defines the word prosper as: to become successful, active, strong, making a lot of money, to favor. The Greek word for prosper means "to carry toward, to bear." The original word "prosper" meant "to grant a prosperous and expeditious journey, to lead by a direct and easy way." Basically you were prosperous if you were on the right path.

So it is with life. Everybody desires to be on the right path and not stray from it, and for the path to be smooth, clear and easy. This is God's desire for us as well, and how we were created to live. Once we make Jesus Lord of our lives and acknowledge him in everything we do, He will direct our paths and make them straight (Prov. 3:5-6).

God never intended for believers to struggle through life. That's why He gave us instructions on how to live prosperously (His Word).

This was another area of our lives where we desperately needed revelation from God! Not trusting God for our finances and failing year after year to seek His will in every decision we made, is what kept us in poverty for the first nine years of our marriage. Although having six children in twelve years grew the level of our financial need over time, it did not represent the root-cause of our financial troubles.

From being on the WIC program at the beginning of our marriage to being on food stamps and government medical assistance for three years, we learned to set our pride aside and receive the help we needed. The government helped pay our electric bill at the beginning of several winters, and my mom helped connect us with an organization that regularly sent us free diapers and baby wipes for three years. We were also able to get free food at a local food bank, along with free clothes for our kids twice a year.

With Jonathan being unemployed for months/years at a time, we even signed up for a program through our church, during one Christmas, where one of the families delivered a tree and a couple of gifts for each of our children. We would not have had a Christmas tree otherwise that year.

Even among all of these struggles, my focus stayed on my Heavenly Father. As I stayed consistent in spending time with my Father, the stress from lack of finances was replaced with peace. God constantly reminded me to dwell on what He had already blessed us with instead of the circumstances that were always glaring at me.

The second part of Third John 2 says that our soul must first prosper before any other area of our lives can prosper. Our mind, will and emotions must be constantly fed and kept in check. This happens when we feed our spirit and keep it in check first. Our spirit is our inner self – our true self. We are a spirit, we have a soul and, during our earthly existence, we live in a body.

Our mind, will and emotions must be constantly fed and kept in check.

These three always operate in this order as seen in the following diagram:

Our mind, like a computer, must be programmed and have constant oversight by a programmer. Our spirit is our programmer that constantly feeds our mind information, either good or bad.

This is why it is so important for us to be aware of what we allow into our eyes and ears, from the persistent noise of the world around us.

It takes discipline to choose to tune our car radio to an uplifting music station. It takes discipline to leave the television off before bed and instead pick up a positive, encouraging book. Even seemingly "innocent" thoughts that come streaming into our mind throughout the day must constantly be vetted. As soon as a thought comes in, we must choose either to leave it there and dwell on it or to cast it out before it develops into a problem.

Our spirit is our programmer that constantly feeds our mind information, either good or bad.

Philippians 4:8 tells us what to think on: Whatever is true, honest, just, pure, lovely, of good report, virtuous and praiseworthy.

So, just like our bodies need proper food and water to be healthy, our spirit needs proper nourishment to be healthy.

Jesus is the bread of life – John 4:14.

When we start each day by feeding our spirit from God's Word and prayer, we will begin to think on these things. They will come to us throughout the day and be of council to us during times of decision.

We must not allow our minds to be controlled by our five senses. This produces a carnal mind. To be carnally minded is to invite distraction and death. To be spiritually minded is to facilitate peace and life!

God has made us one with Himself - a glorious revelation (John 17:21). His Spirit is our reborn Spirit and we also have the mind of Christ (1 Cor. 2:16).

With the Holy Spirit being our teacher, then can we learn every day who we are, and the authority we were created to walk in. Romans 12:1-2 encourages us to "not be conformed to this world; but be transformed by the renewing of your mind that you may prove what is that good and acceptable and perfect will of God."

The MSG version explains perfectly God's heart in this! "So, this is the simple process for those who wish to live a prosperous life. Prosperous in every area… spiritually, physically, financially, emotionally, socially…"

It is only after we get to this point that we will be able to help those around us. This world we live in is in desperate need of mature believers, who will stand up and take initiative to solve the many problems this world is facing.

It's not the job of the government to do this. The church must rise up and take its place in this day of restoration. God has given us the ministry of reconciliation, according to 2 Cor. 5:19-20. Our mission in Jesus' name is to reconcile the world to Himself. God has committed unto us the word of reconciliation. To reconcile is to renew the relationship.

Wasn't this our Father's heart since the moment Adam broke fellowship with God in the Garden of Eden? To restore the intimate relationship they had? To restore being able to walk hand in hand with our Creator in the cool of the morning, lost in deep conversations?

Conversations about what to create next, how to understand the breadth and length and depth and height of our Father's love, the intricate plans of bringing Heaven to this Earth. Once our relationship with our Father is restored we are to restore relationships with each other.

Some other things that the Father has that belong to us:

Colossians 1:19 tells us, "In Jesus all the fullness of God dwells."

Matt. 28:18 says, All power was given to Jesus.

John 1:16 -- Of Jesus' fullness have we all received, and Grace for grace. The Greek reads, "Grace upon Grace" (gifts piled on top of each other).

John 3:35 and Ephesians 1:23 also expound on how we are filled with God's fullness. What a powerful revelation!

The fullness of God dwells in Jesus, which means the fullness of Jesus dwells in us. And on top of that fullness are gifts piled up on top of each other. It would be enough to just be filled with all the fullness of God, but then the icing on the cake is the extra gifts and graces piled up high.

What a loving Father we have!

How he desires to lavish His gifts upon us (Eph. 1:6, 7-8 AMP)! Lavish is the nature of our God. Lavish in love, mercy, goodness…

Lavish is the nature of our God.

Ephesians 2:7 calls it "the incomparable riches of God's grace" (NIV). The words incomparable and exceeding mean "thrown beyond the normal mark." It seems God is never at a loss at how to describe His marvelous attributes!

Chapter 13

Made Alive

Another precious promise from the heart of our Heavenly Father is that He will quicken us when we spend time in His Word (Ps. 119:25, Ps. 143:11, Heb. 4:12).

The word quicken means: To make alive, to revive, to communicate a principle of grace to. From the Old Testament to the New Testament, the word quicken is used to describe how God made us alive when we were dead in sins (Eph. 2).

Another definition of quicken is "to hasten, to accelerate, to sharpen, to stimulate, to refresh by new supplies of comfort and grace" (Ps. 119). Hebrews 4:12 confirms the dictionary definition of quicken as "to make sharper" when it tells us that the Word of God is sharper than any two-edged sword, piercing to the division of soul and spirit, of joints and marrow and discerning the thoughts and intentions of the heart.

All we have to do is simply put God's Word in our eyes and ears, so that it gets down in our hearts and begins to shape who we are. It will then come out of our mouths.

Instead of being conformed to this world we will begin to be transformed! Jeremiah 23:29 says that God's Word is like a fire and like a hammer that breaks the rock in pieces.

Who wouldn't want to be made alive? There sure is enough death, sickness and defeat in this world. People are crying out for some light to shine in their lives and to feel alive.

David prayed in Psalm 119:40 -- "Quicken me in your righteousness" and in Psalm 119:88 "Quicken me after your loving-kindness." How about this

Instead of being conformed to this world we will begin to be transformed!

revelation: Romans 8:11 -- "The same Spirit that raised Jesus from the dead dwells in us." That Spirit will quicken our mortal bodies.

How many men and women wish their bodies were better, healthier, in better shape, more toned, or smoother skinned? Glamour Health presented a survey that 97 percent of women admitted at least once every day they felt that they hated their bodies. Our western culture has put unnecessary pressure on people, especially on women starting as young as seven years old. This lie in our culture must be fought with God's Word. As parents we must teach our children that they are the body of Christ and how to put on Christ daily. When we walk after the Spirit and not after the flesh, our focus will shift from how we look physically to how we're growing spiritually and how we're feeding and nourishing God himself within us.

After all, we are made in His image and we will only operate at our best when we're nourishing ourselves properly. It becomes easy to resist negative influences when our spirit is constantly being fed with God's Word.

This process works the same way when it comes to feeding our physical bodies. Dr. Don Colbert is an excellent resource for learning how to eat, according to God's plan for us.

Every believer deep down longs for a more intimate relationship with their Heavenly Father. People want somewhere to belong, something to contribute to.

What else does our Father have that belongs to us? We must realize that God has already blessed us with everything that He is and has (Eph. 1:1-3). Not, "He's going to …" He already has!

How do we walk in these blessings every day? All we need to do is understand that every blessing is already ours. Once we believe with all our hearts that it's ours, we will take it and expect it to operate in our lives.

What we expect to happen is what happens all the time! We expect that our oven will start to heat up when we are ready to make dinner, so we don't think twice about turning the knob to turn it on. If we hesitated, we would have doubts that it would turn on. Those doubts usually come from already knowing that something was wrong with it.

Thank God there never has to be any form of doubt in using what God has given us, because there has never been a time when what He has given us has failed or malfunctioned in any way. Why would we doubt the ability of something to work, unless we had experienced some kind of fault in it?

Knowing who God is and always will be strengthens our confidence that everything He's given us will always work 100% of the time. God is not a man that He should lie (Num. 23:19).

God is Love. Love covers a multitude of sins. When we walk around, knowing from the bottom of our hearts that we are free from all sin and full of God's love, we can freely focus on how God is working through us every day. But first we must lose sight of ourselves and even lose sight of those around us, until we can only see God and walk in the anticipation of what He is going to do and how He is going to work.

When God is our focus, self-focus (self-consciousness) disappears. When God is our focus, it becomes hard to focus on others' faults and imperfections. We will be free to minister effectively when our only focus is God and His love.

I love how the MSG puts Matthew 10:39. "If your first concern is to look after yourself, you'll never find yourself. But if you forget about yourself and look to Me, you'll find both yourself and Me."

What we focus on is what grows in us. Matthew 22:37-40 is our greatest calling – 1: to Love the Lord our God with all our hearts and with all our souls and with all our minds, and 2: to love each other as we do ourselves (after all, each of us manifests the image of God).

Intimacy with God has no contenders. No earthly romantic love will ever be able to exceed an intimate love relationship with God. And God likes it this way! In Exodus 34:14, He says He is jealous for our affection.

What we focus on is what grows in us.

The more we dwell on everything our Father has supplied us with, the more we will believe that those things are actually ours and we will become extremely excited to use those gifts and graces.

It will become a way of life! And to think of not accepting and using everything that our Father has given us would be to us like rejecting the sacrifice of Jesus on the cross for us. Jesus came that we might have life and have it more abundantly.

If He only came that we may have life, that would be exciting enough, but He came to provide us with abundant life (John 10:10). "Life to the full, till it overflows!"

We show our true love for Jesus when we accept and walk in every single thing He provided for us, through His death on the cross. "In Him we live and move and have our being" (Acts. 17:28). I love verses 26 & 27 in the MSG! "He doesn't play hide-and-seek with us. He's not remote; He's near."

It's time to flush religion and its constrictive rules and regulations and begin living in God's grace. My favorite definition of Grace, as revealed to Kenneth Copeland by God is, "God's overwhelming desire to treat you and me as if sin had never happened."

What an amazing way to live! What a freeing lifestyle! Never walking on eggshells, wondering if we're good enough. Never wondering if we're doing enough good things to stay in God's graces. No lists of rules to keep.

Our only focus is upon Jesus and each other, keeping the two great commandments He gave us in Luke 10:27, Matthew 22:37 and Mark 12:30-31.

So many believers continue to keep the Old Testament law in front of them. 1 Timothy 1:9 clearly explains that the law was not laid down for the just, but for the lawless and disobedient – in short, the sinners!

"He doesn't play hide-and-seek with us. He's not remote; He's near."

The law is not there to fix our sin but to reveal sin and our need for Jesus. Imagine having a big zit on your face, and you grab a mirror to inspect it. After cringing and realizing it *is* as bad as you thought, you take the mirror and start rubbing it on your face, hoping it will heal the zit! Who does that? Nobody. We know the mirror is only there to reveal the problem, not to fix it.

So it is with the Old Testament law. It is meant to be only a mirror, to reveal our faults so we can look to Jesus to receive our cleansing and perfecting.

Romans 8:1-2 reminds us "So now there is no condemnation for those who belong to Christ Jesus." Hebrews 8:12 reiterates, "And I (God) will forgive their wickedness, and I will never again remember their sins."

In Exodus 34:7, God said, "I do not excuse the guilty. I lay the sins of the parents upon their children and grandchildren; the entire family is affected -- even children in the third and fourth generations." Praise God this was the truth *before* the cross and praise Jesus that Hebrews 8:12 is our truth *now!*

If any book claims to exhaust the subject of God's grace of gifts, I would question the author's honesty and humility. It is not humanly possible to fully grasp everything that our Father has given us. How exciting though to know that every day, as we spend time with Him, He reveals more of His heart to us and His overwhelming desire for us to know Him more intimately. Like any earthly relationship, the more time invested in it, the more it will grow and the more you learn about that person.

The more time we spend with our Father, the brighter our path gets. "The path of the just is as the shining light, that shines more and more unto the perfect day" (Prov. 4:18).

The more time we spend with our Father, the brighter our path gets.

God's grace is so rich, so limitless. It is rich and is lavished on us, abounding toward us. More than what is needed, above what is necessary! Ephesians 2:7 tells us more about this super-abundant grace or gifts. The NIV says "exceeding riches."

Jesus has already paid the price for us to walk in everything that God has given us. It's up to us to receive these gifts, beginning with Jesus' free gift of salvation.

If you've never received this free gift simply pray:

Heavenly Father, in the Name of Jesus, I present myself to you.

I pray and ask Jesus to be Lord over my life. I believe it in my heart, so I say it with my mouth: "Jesus has been raised from the dead." This moment, I make Him the Lord over my life.

Jesus, come into my heart. I believe this moment that I am saved, I say it now: "I am reborn. I am a Christian. I am a child of Almighty God."

Now, thank God for making you His child. Colossians 1:12 says, "Giving thanks unto the Father, which hath made us meet to be partakers of the inheritance of the saints in light." You have just been made a partaker of an inheritance from God. **You have just inherited the kingdom of God!**

Speaking of God, the next verse says, "Who hath delivered us from the power of darkness, and hath translated us into the kingdom of his dear Son: In whom we have the redemption through his blood, even the forgiveness of sins."

You don't have to wait until you die to receive your inheritance. You are a child of God right this very moment, and you can receive all that belongs to you right now!

1 John 3:2 says, "Beloved, **now** are we the sons of God." You have been delivered from the darkness into the kingdom of God.

Jesus said, "Fear not, little flock; for it is your Father's good pleasure to give you the kingdom" (Luke 12:32).

- See more at: http://www.kcm.org/real-help/salvation/learn/how-become-a-christian#sthash.Esm3KUge.dpuf

Once we receive God's free gift of salvation and His Holy Spirit, our eyes will be opened to these gifts, and then as Proverbs 17:8 says, whichever way we turn these gifts in our hands, they will prosper us.

1 Timothy 4:14-15 reminds us to not neglect the gifts you have; practicing them and immersing ourselves in them. 2 Timothy 1:6 reiterates for us to "Fan into flame the gift of God in us."

One morning I came across this verse while spending time with the Lord. 1 Timothy 4:14 says "Do not neglect the spiritual gift you received through the prophecy spoken over you when the elders of the church laid their hands on you."

I was immediately reminded that a few years ago somebody prophesied a spirit of Deborah over me. I had neglected and almost forgotten this gift that was given to me through prophecy. I decided to meditate on this word so that I would prosper through it, making it visible in everything I do and to everyone I meet, as verse fifteen from this passage says. When I continue in this word, I will be saved and those who hear me will be saved, according to verse sixteen.

I went to Judges 4 and 5 to read the story of Deborah the Judge. An interesting thing I had never seen before about Deborah was that she had a husband! She was a wife, mother, political leader, poetess, prophetess, judge and singer. She was a warrior!

I found out that the name Deborah means "Bee." A bee has two characteristics. Something sweet -- honey, and something powerful -- a sting. What a beautiful combination... this *is* the Spirit of Deborah!

Another prominent quality of bees is unity. Bees are classified as "families" and always work in unity. The "sweet" that the spirit of Deborah produces will be evident to all. Others will "taste and see that the Lord is good" (Ps. 34:8, 2 Cor. 2:15).

In the Bible, Deborah chose to go with Barak to battle when Barak displayed fear of going alone. But even as Deborah went, she stayed in her role and let Barak stay in his. As a result they could rejoice together in the victory. They were able to sing a song of victory together after God defeated the enemy for them.

Help others accomplish a goal for the furthering of God's Kingdom, not for selfish gain.

Here's something even more interesting... we see Barak's name in the "Hall of Faith" in Hebrews 11 but not Deborah's name; although without Deborah, Barak would not have even been mentioned!

That's an example of a true spirit of unity. Helping others accomplish a goal for the furthering of God's Kingdom, not for selfish gain. Each of us as believers and members of the body of Christ play a vital role in completing the body every day.

The Word of God also has these two characteristics:

Psalm 119:103 – "How sweet your words taste to me; they are sweeter than honey."

Hebrews 4:12 – "For the word of God is alive and powerful. It is sharper than the sharpest two-edged sword, cutting between soul and spirit, between joint and marrow. It exposes our innermost thoughts and desires."

What a powerful revelation of the spirit of Deborah that is upon me and working through me. I receive it and endeavor to cultivate it.

It is also interesting that the only Deborahs mentioned in the Bible were Deborah the judge, and Deborah, Rebekah's nursemaid. The nursemaid exudes a sweet, nurturing spirit. My prayer is that every day these two characteristics are developed in me to create a perfectly balanced, peaceful warrior. Just as a duck glides serenely above the surface of a lake, unseen below are those feet, kicking furiously!

Another gift God has given us is angels (Ps. 103:20-21).

How do we receive everything God has given us? By faith. This sounds like such a simple answer, and it is! Praise God, that through the simplicity of faith, even a small child can understand and receive His gifts.

It's interesting how James and John in Mark 10:35-40 asked Jesus if they could sit with Him on His throne. Jesus responded that it wasn't He who decided that, but God Himself, who has prepared the places for His chosen ones. Well, we are His chosen ones! Ephesians 2:6 explains that "God has raised us up together and made us sit together in heavenly places in Christ Jesus."

I've been seeking God to find out where our four oldest children will go to school in the fall. We know without a doubt that they need to go to a different school, but after praying on and off for a few weeks, we had no direction on where they should go. We only knew they needed to be in a Christian school.

Finally after asking the same question "Where do You want our children to go to school," I heard in my spirit that I was asking the wrong question. God said what I should be asking is, "What is Your heart for our children?" So I asked that and He said, "To spend time with them in a place undisturbed."

Our home needs to be the central place where we train them up for God and build that foundation. It's up to us where we send them to school, based on God's Word, but our teaching at home really needs to improve.

I felt led to find out exactly what God's Word says about education. In my search, I found:

Jesus grew in wisdom as he grew in stature (Luke 2:52).

I found that Proverbs exhorts a son to heed his father's instruction, and that in applying it, discovers wisdom.

Proper, Biblical education begins with the parent and child at home (Eph. 6:4).

I found that the basis of all true knowledge is the reverence of the Lord (Prov. 1:7).

I saw in John 8:32 that freedom from fear comes from being educated in Truth and that our knowledge of God informs every other area of our lives (Rom. 6:11-13).

I saw that knowledge, apart from the love of God, leads to pride (1 Cor. 8:1). How true this is!

I found that as we study God's Word, we become more equipped for God's work (2 Tim. 3:7 and 2 Peter 3:18).

After receiving all this revelation, I decided to listen to a message on the KCM website, something I do almost every day to strengthen my spirit. I happened to select a message where, at the end, Kenneth Copeland prayed for people and called out certain requests, one of them being education!

"Whatever we need is in the seed, which is in us"

My eyes became glued to my phone as Kenneth said, "Whatever we need is in the seed, which is in us. Not only will you have the money to pay for it, but go back and re-pray about where they're supposed to go to school. If we will listen to God and do what He tells us and send them where He says send them, it's already taken care of. It's already done!"

My heart overflowed with thankfulness at how my Father is constantly pursuing me! I immediately went back to God's Word and asked Him where He wants our children to go to school. I still wanted to find a specific verse with unmistakable instructions. Right then a specific verse started running through my head. I looked it up and the name of the school was in this verse! I couldn't have received any clearer instruction!

God also told me that "Immediate obedience prevents hardness of heart." It's so important to take action right away on instructions God gives us, even if we can't see the whole picture yet. We're excited to see how God is going to supply the means for our children to go to school this fall. Whatever way/ways He supplies, it will be a testimony to him that we will share with others.

How do we receive everything that God has given us? Like a child (Mark 10:15). Anyone who has children understands that they don't have any problem receiving what is given to them! They will even ask for more after they have just been given something.

A child understands the love of his parents and automatically assumes they will be given what they need and want. And they are usually persistent in asking until they get what they want! When we understand how much our Father loves us and desires for us to receive everything He's given us, it will be easy for us to receive it and activate it in our lives. The more we believe His love, the more we will receive His luxuries. Not just the bare necessities to get through life, but *abundance*!

"God's blessing makes life rich; nothing we do can improve on God" (Prov. 10:22).

Chapter 14

Desire to Be a Giver

So what belongs to us as believers?

Outside of being empowered to love like God does, the greatest gift our Father has given us is the ability to give.

I vividly remember the day I was listening to Kenneth Copeland teach on why we work. I always thought we work so that we have money to live; but Ephesians 4:28 clearly states, that we work so that we

We don't work to live; we work to give!

have resources to give to those in need. We don't work to live; we work to give!

As I continued to study God's principles for living, I saw that first and foremost we were to tithe (give back to God ten percent of our increase). Jonathan and I knew, from day one of our marriage, that we were commanded to be tithers. Over the years though, as our finances went from bad to worse, we ended up tithing very sporadically, when we thought we had extra to do so.

We knew one of the reasons we weren't increasing was because we weren't tithing regularly. You would think we would just take God at His Word, since one benefit of tithing is that He will rebuke Satan for our sakes. Unfortunately though, stubbornness and fear of lack controlled our lives for nine years.

The end of the summer of 2015 rolled around, and we were so sick of living in lack and poverty. Our two-bedroom, one and one-half bathroom, 1,200 sq. ft. townhome was suffocating our family of eight! Every day for months, I searched for homes for rent so we could move, but everything I found was too expensive, considering Jonathan was unemployed again.

One hot July day that summer, Jonathan spent significant time seeking God to find answers on how to move forward in life. He knew he was a good guy, but God spoke to him, saying that just being a good guy didn't please God. It was faith in Him. Faith coming from spending regular time in His Word, seeking him for every decision.

The number one decision God told Jonathan to make was to tithe regularly. So, even though he couldn't see how we could give ten percent of what little money we had coming in from his unemployment check, he decided we would tithe regularly. We began tithing, committing to God that we would *never* compromise in that area again. EVER!

Just a few weeks later, three different employers lined up interviews for Jonathan. He received and accepted an offer on one of those jobs. Now Jonathan makes more money per year than he ever has in his life, AND with the potential for big year-end bonuses, every year!

Finally, we were in a position to consider purchasing our first home! We immediately contacted a realtor friend of ours to start the process right away!

One of the first things we discovered was that we had no credit at all. Not necessarily bad credit, but no credit. This was due to the fact that we never had any credit cards or loans over the past seven years. This would mean settling on a home would take about six months. As soon as I heard that, something inside told me we would definitely be moving by the end of the year. I could see us moving, and refused to accept a different timeline!

Miraculously, opportunities to overcome our circumstances were immediately placed in our path. Our credit score became perfect four weeks later! Finally, we were approved for a loan big enough for a home that would fit our family. Two months later, right before Christmas, we signed all the papers -- and became first time homeowners; the whole process having taken three months instead of six!

With Jonathan working hard at his new job and traveling almost every week, I was the one who completely packed up for the big move (which I was fine with). On the day of New Year's eve, we moved into our new home!

We now live in a gorgeous two-story home within a peaceful neighborhood, surrounded by beautiful views. It is located just a few houses from the end of a cul-de-sac, the safe environment we always envisioned for our children.

Our ten-year-old home includes five bedrooms, four full bathrooms, a 2-car garage and even a basketball net in the driveway! We didn't even have to buy any of the appliances, since the refrigerator and dishwasher came with the home, and Jonathan's parents graciously bought us a beautiful huge washer and dryer set as our Christmas present!

This was the answer to our prayers, and a dream-come-true! However, the door to this blessing would have taken a lot longer to open, had we not decided to tithe regularly. And now, seven months later, we have never missed a week of tithing and never will again!

God desires to expand our capacity to live by all of His words.

God desires to expand our capacity to live by all of His words. We can do this when we allow Him to energize us with His power (Eph. 3:16). It's by faith so that it might be by grace.

When we're rooted and grounded in love, people will know it. We are filled with *all* the fullness of God, but first we must understand that we have the name of God.

Who is God to us?

- Our Father
- Our Financier
- Our Healer – Ex.15:26
- Our Deliverer – Ps. 34:4 &7
- Our Protector
- Our Lover
- Our Forgiver
- Our Judge – Deut. 20:4, Ex. 34:5-7, Ps. 50:6
- Our Encourager – Matt. 25:21
- Our Teacher – Matt. 28:18
- Our Rewarder – Heb. 11:6
- Our Hiding Place – Deut. 33:27
- Our Rock – 2 Sam. 22:32-34
- Our Planner – Ps. 33:11-13
- Our Lawyer – Ps. 37:31
- Our Guide – Ps. 48:14
- Our Salvation – Ps. 62:7, Ex. 15:2, Isa. 12:2
- Our Shield – Ps. 84:11, Prov. 30:5
- Our Builder and maker – Heb. 11:16
- Our Song Leader – Ex. 15:2
- Our King – Ps. 47:2 & 7

- Our Source – Rom. 8:32
- Our Miracle worker – Gal. 3:5
- Our Covenant Maker – Heb. 10:16
- Our Light – James 1:17
- Our Comforter – 2 Cor. 1:3
- Our Bread of Life – John 6:48-58
- Our Counselor – Isa. 9:6
- Our Foundation – Isa. 28:16

Just as a woman takes the man's last name in marriage, making the two of them one, so too we become one with God, when we take His name and become part of His family.

When we are filled with the fullness of God, there won't be any room for bitterness, unforgiveness or negative conversation (Eph. 4:31).

We are to give no place to the devil for the sake of the anointing (Eph. 4:27). God's anointing in us pushes out the devil's lies.

Living as givers will ensure that every area of our lives will prosper. The beginning of living a prosperous life is to inquire of God, concerning exactly where He wants us to work, play, sow, etc.

When what we are doing lines up with God's assignments for us, life will be smooth. We will take our commands from our commander in chief, God, and operate in the army of the Lord; all the while taking great delight in His commands (Ps. 112:1).

There are different facets associated with each of our assignments, just like a diamond is one jewel but has many facets.

Each assignment puts us in alignment with the body of Christ (our diamond); however, there are many facets of approach to this same goal. Each of us gets to take one, that we may contribute to the whole of His body.

Sometimes a husband and wife will each have assignments that differ from the other, but as believers, the "diamond" is always the same – "Go ye into all the world and preach the gospel to every creature."

We are the light to shine in the darkness. When the world is against our beliefs is the time we need to shine the brightest. Like Josiah, we must grab God's Word and run with it, never looking to the right or left.

> **We are lights to shine in the darkness.**

In John 15:15 Jesus said, "All things that I have heard of my Father I have made known unto you." That's Huge!

What are other gifts that our Father has given us?

God has given us the gift of prophesying, serving, teaching, encouraging, giving, leading, and showing mercy (Rom. 12:4-8).

Other gifts are Faith, healing, miraculous powers, distinguishing between spirits, speaking in different tongues and interpreting tongues (1 Cor. 12:9-11).

We must be faithful stewards of the graces (gifts) God has given us. We do this by serving others. Our speech matching God's

Word, and everything we accomplish happening through the strength God provides (1 Peter 4:10-11).

God is so loyal to His faithful… God keeps covenant with them that love Him and keep His commandments, even to a thousand generations (Deut. 7:9). That's a long time!

He will bless us, and multiply us; bless our children and our work, and God will take all sickness and disease away from us.

Our Father sent His Word and it healed us. What a wonderful way to live! Every area of lives whole and walking in all of the gifts God has given us.

My prayer for you is to take a firm grip upon this revelation and to own it! Do this by opening yourself to first receive all the gifts we have access to as believers. Then together, we can go forth with these gifts and be the change this world so desperately needs!